This Book Belongs to

Lilie ofc

Thank you for your purchase.

**To ensure that you have the best experience using this coloring book and to prevent bleeding, although the illustrations are on one-side, we highly recommend coloring using pencils.
If you are going to use any kind of ink that may cause bleeding throughout the papers, we recommend tearing out the coloring pages or using a buffer page. (you can find blank buffer pages at the end of the book.)**

Copyright
All original work rights reserved. This book or any portion of it may not be reproduced or used in any manner whatsoever without the express written permission of the author & the publisher except for the use of brief quotations in a book review.
Licensed graphics used with all appropriate commercial licenses.
Although, the publisher and author have used their best efforts in writing and preparing this book, they make no representations or warranties with respect to the accuracy or completeness of the contents of this document. The information is to be used at your own risk. The author cannot guarantee any specific outcomes that may result from using the methods outlined in the following pages.

With only one color to fill the spiral or the zigzag lines, you'll reveal a cute dog or a puppy picture!

45 Coloring pages (15 spirals, 15 zigzag lines and 15 dots).

Fill in between the lines with only one color, either going spiral or in zigzag lines or dots to reveal the final picture.

Some few pictures might be a mystery while in others you might be able to guess the animal before starting to color.

You can find a gallery of the pictures at the end of the book.

Don't worry about going outside the lines, the lines are forgiving and when you finish coloring, you may see the animal art you created better if you look at the picture from three to five feet away (1-1.5 meter) away.

Where to start coloring?

For the spiral coloring pages:

Start coloring by filling in the lines from outside as shown here.

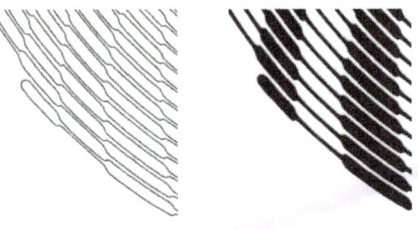

For the zigzag coloring pages:

Start coloring by filling in the lines from upper lines or the lower line as shown here.

For the dots coloring pages:

Start coloring by filling inside the dots.

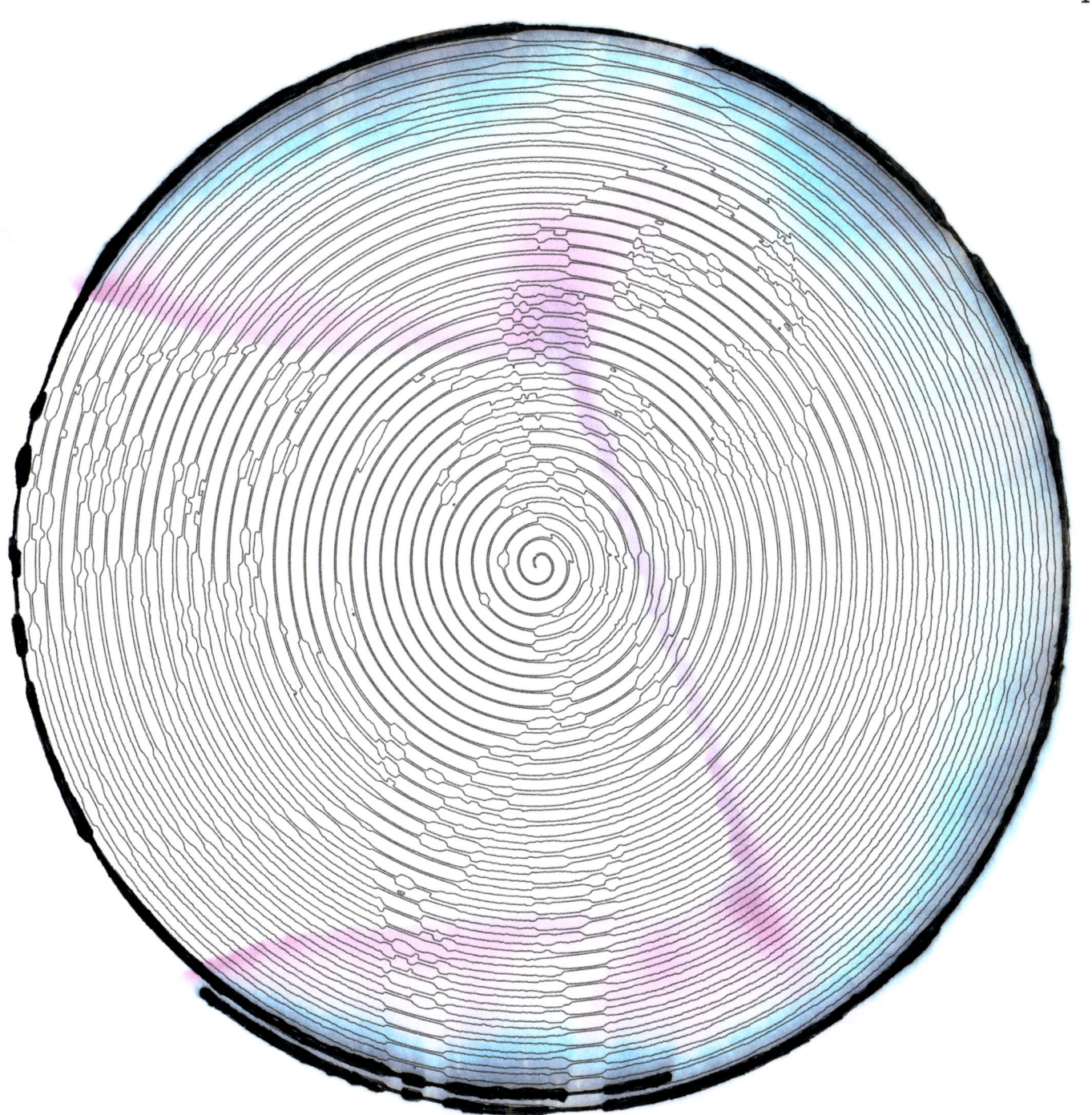

1

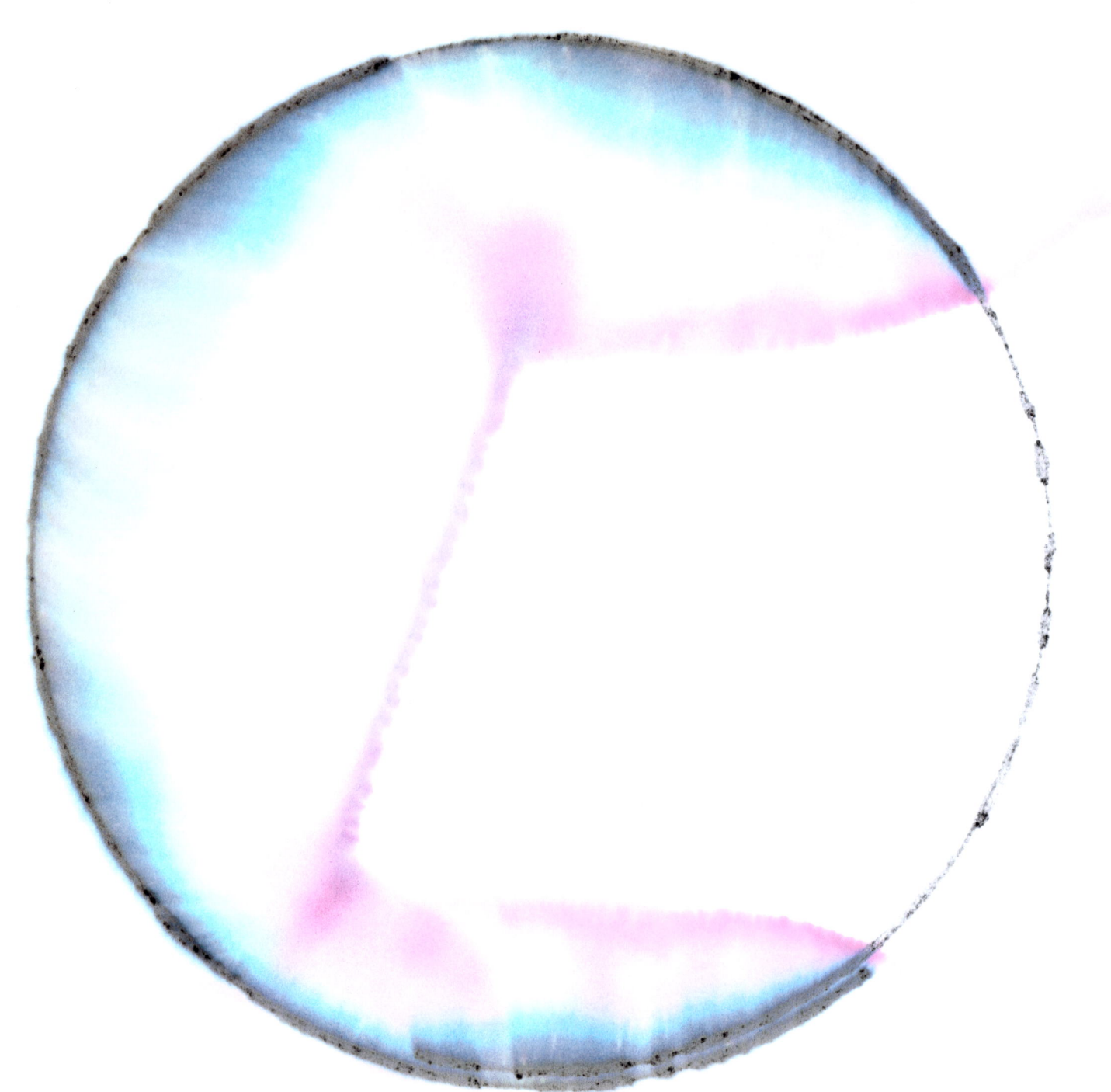
This page is intentionally left blank to prevent color bleed.

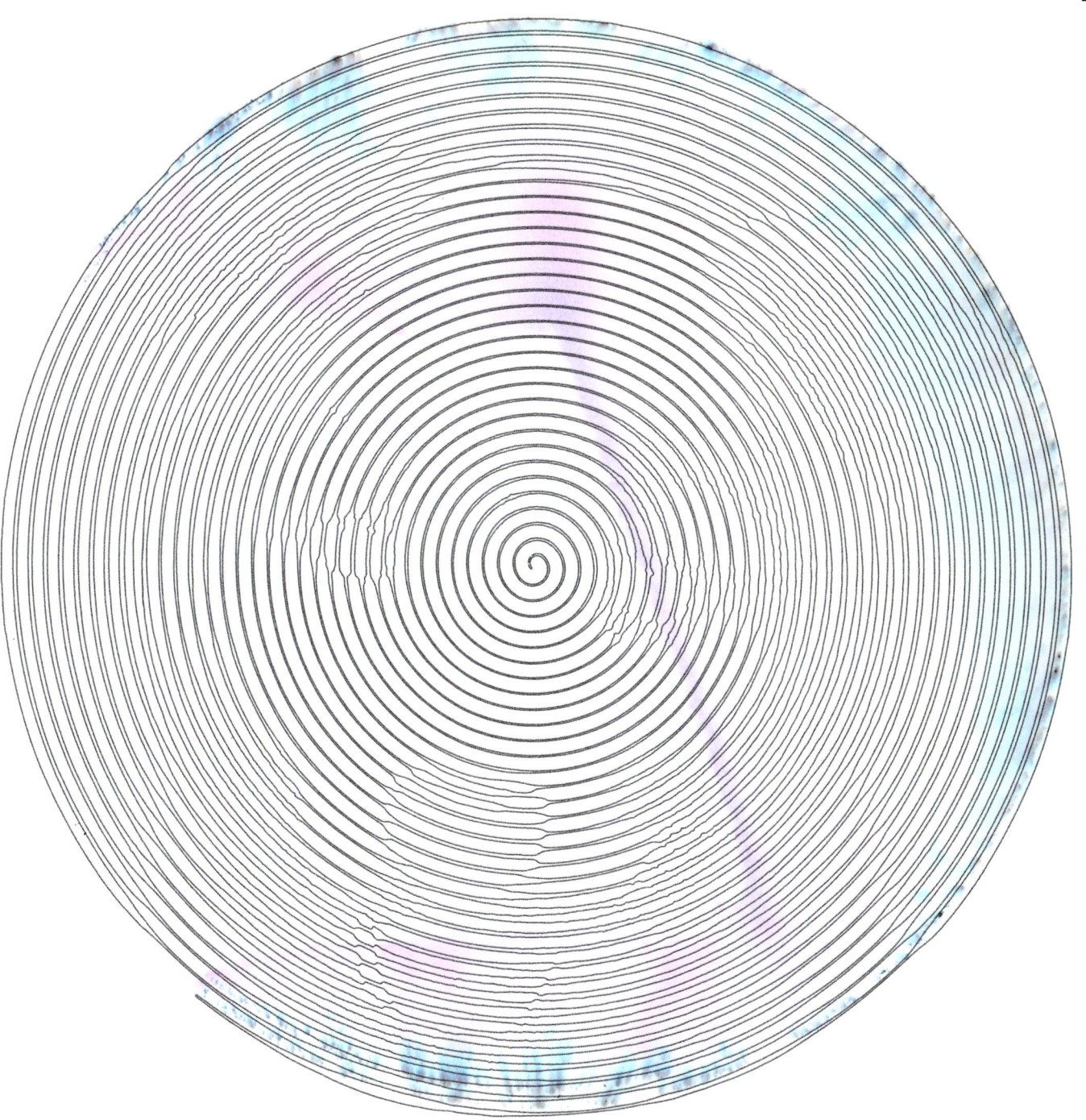

This page is intentionally left blank to prevent color bleed.

3

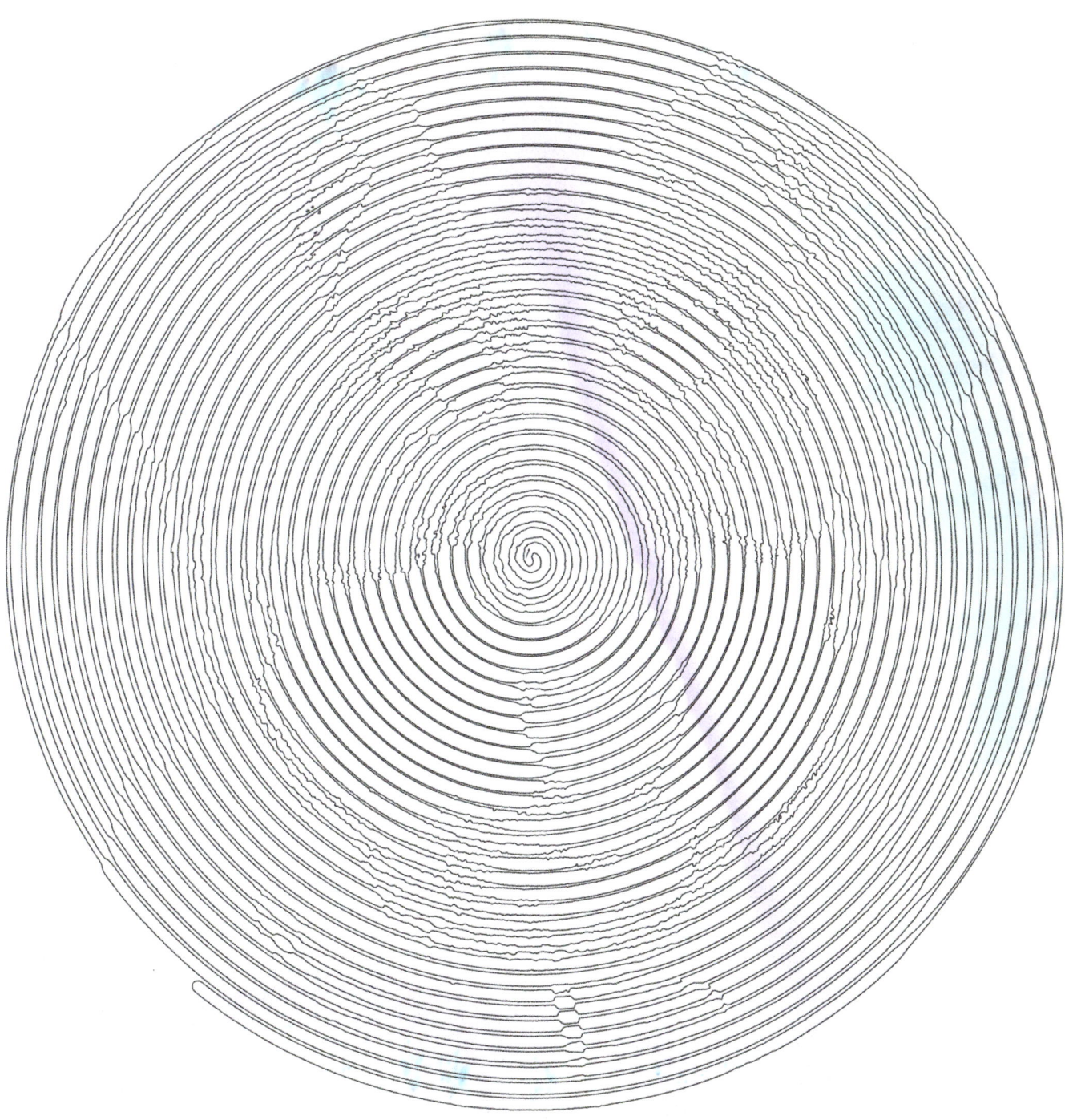

This page is inte ntionally left blank to prevent color bleed.

4

This page is intentionally left blank to prevent color bleed.

This page is intentionally left blank to prevent color bleed.

This page is intentionally left blank to prevent color bleed.

This page is intentionally left blank to prevent color bleed.

This page is intentionally left blank to prevent color bleed.

11

This page is intentionally left blank to prevent color bleed.

13

This page is intentionally left blank to prevent color bleed.

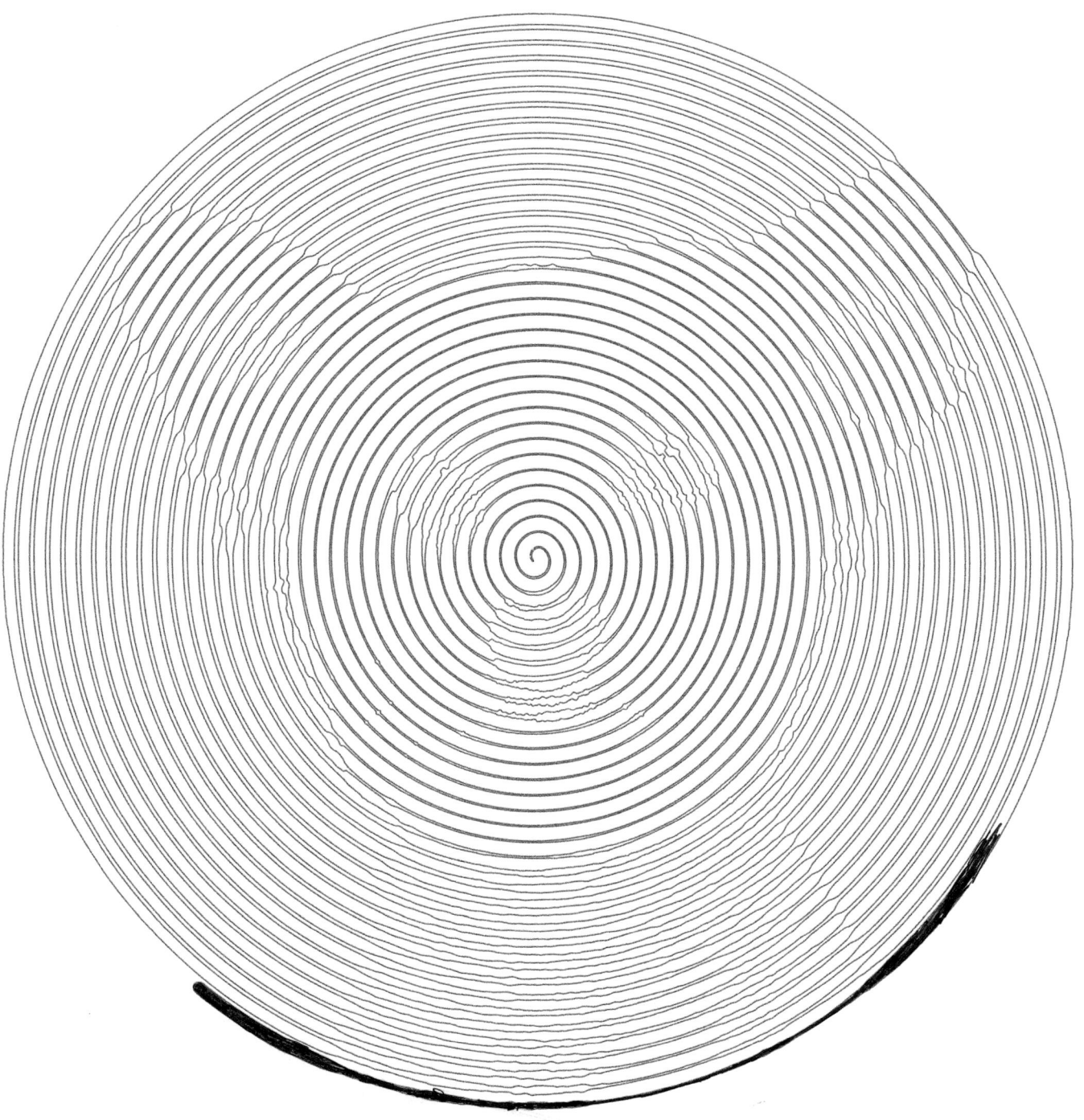

This page is intentionally left blank to prevent color bleed.

15

2

3

4

5

6

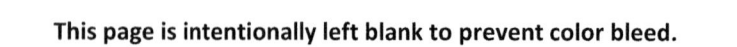

7

8

This page is intentionally left blank to prevent color bleed.

9

This page is intentionally left blank to prevent color bleed.

10

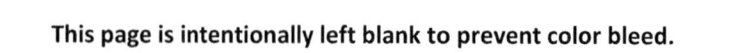

11

12

This page is intentionally left blank to prevent color bleed.

13

14

15

1

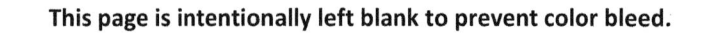

2

3

4

This page is intentionally left blank to prevent color bleed.

5

This page is intentionally left blank to prevent color bleed.

6

7

This page is intentionally left blank to prevent color bleed.

8

This page is intentionally left blank to prevent color bleed.

9

This page is intentionally left blank to prevent color bleed.

10

11

This page is intentionally left blank to prevent color bleed.

12

This page is intentionally left blank to prevent color bleed.

13

This page is intentionally left blank to prevent color bleed.

14

15

This page is intentionally left blank to prevent color bleed.

1

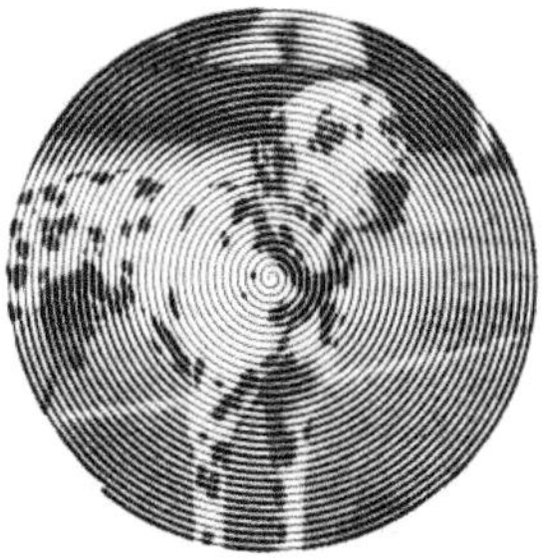

2

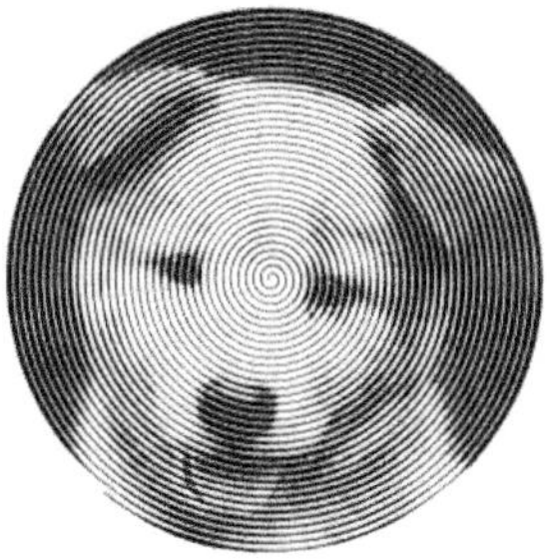

3

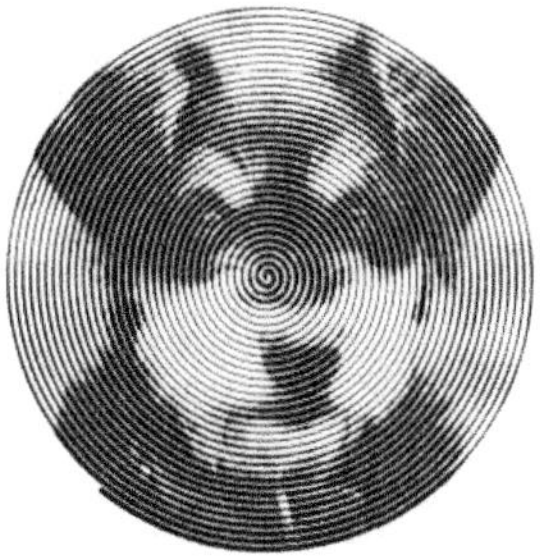

4

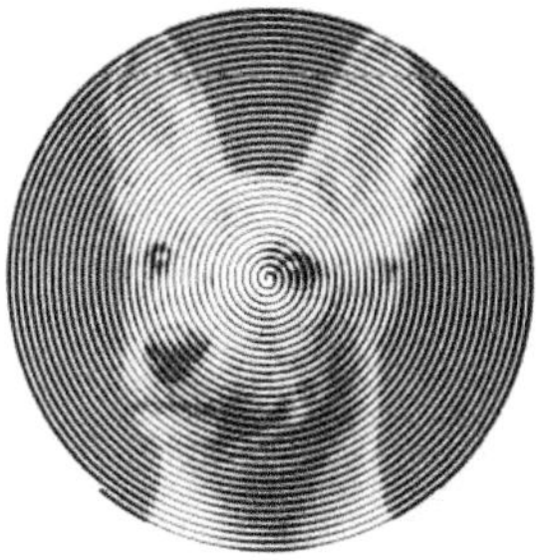

5

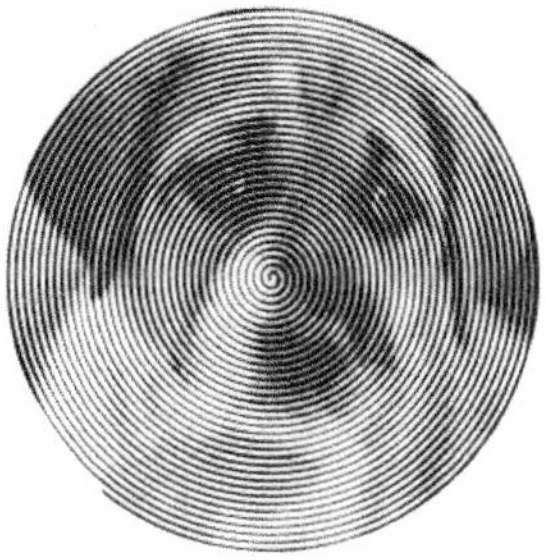

6

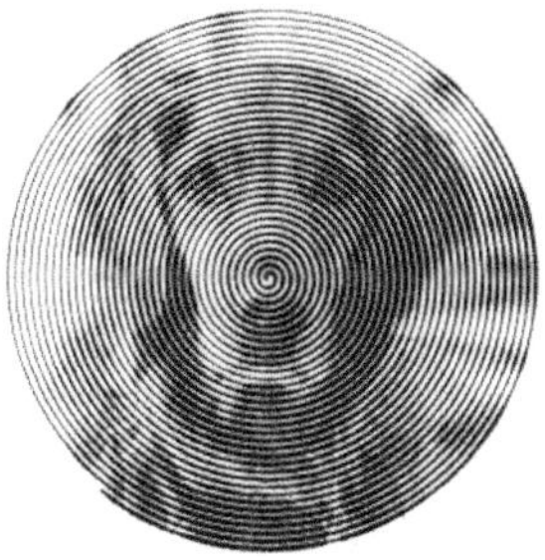

7

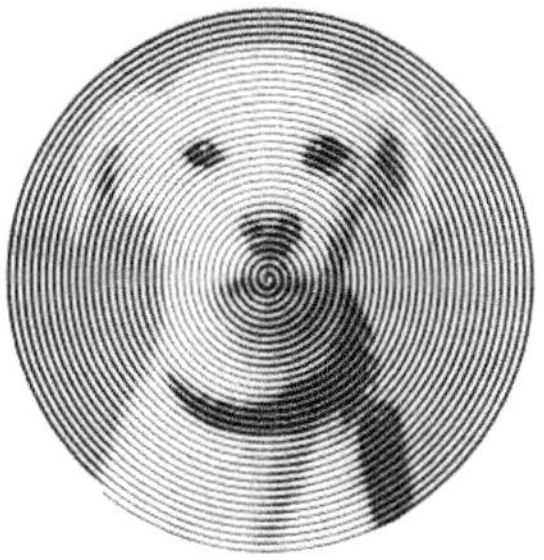

8

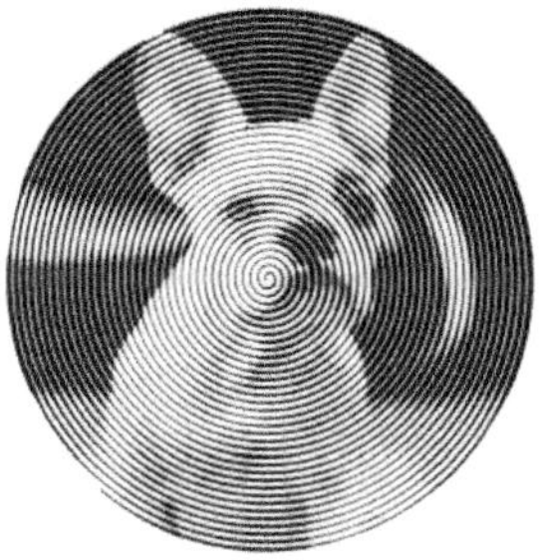

9

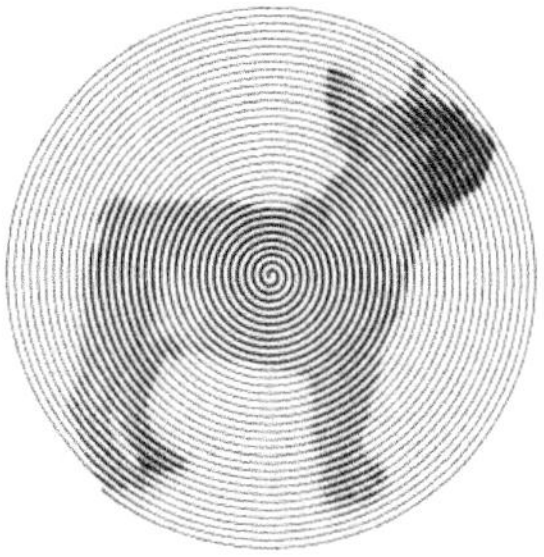

10

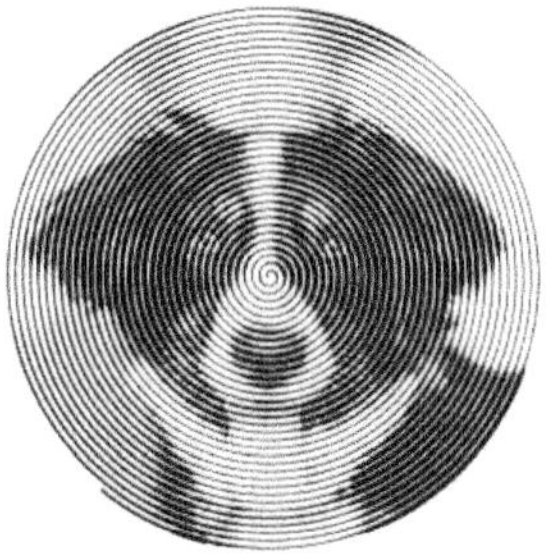

11

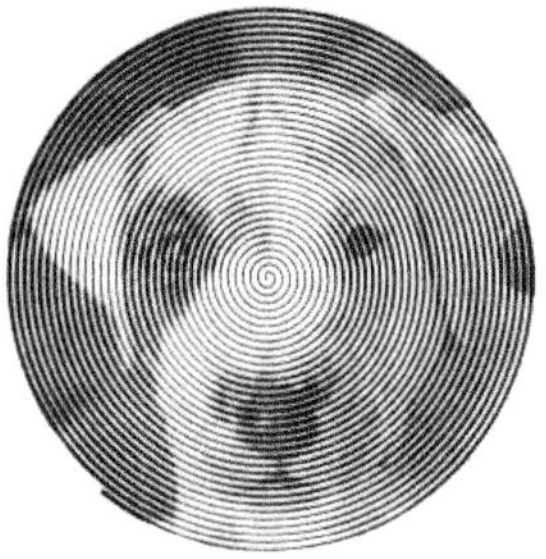

12

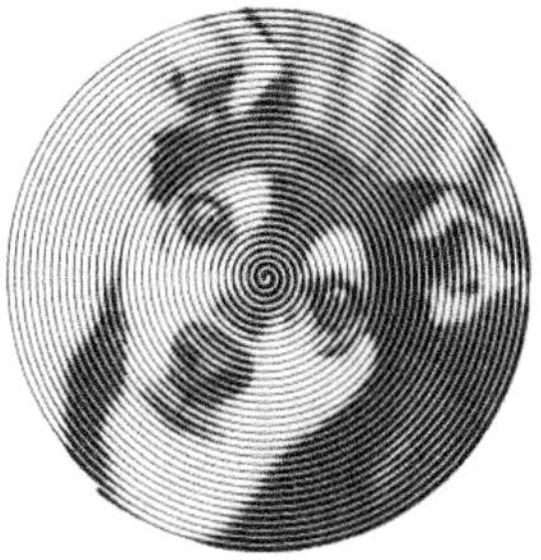

13

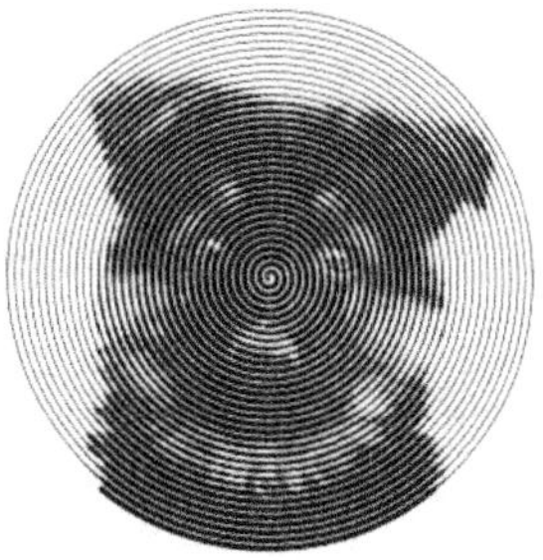

14

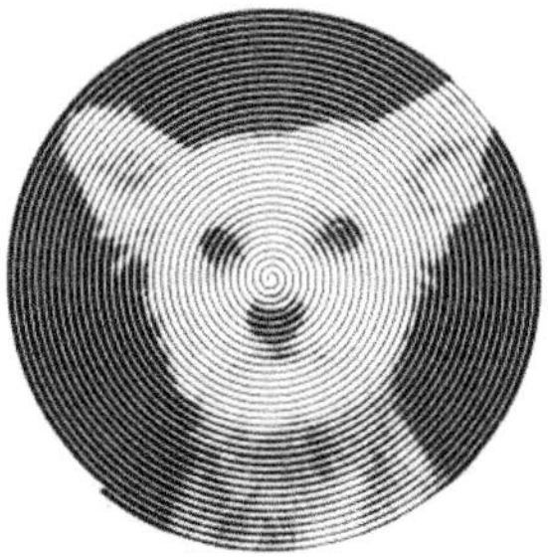

15

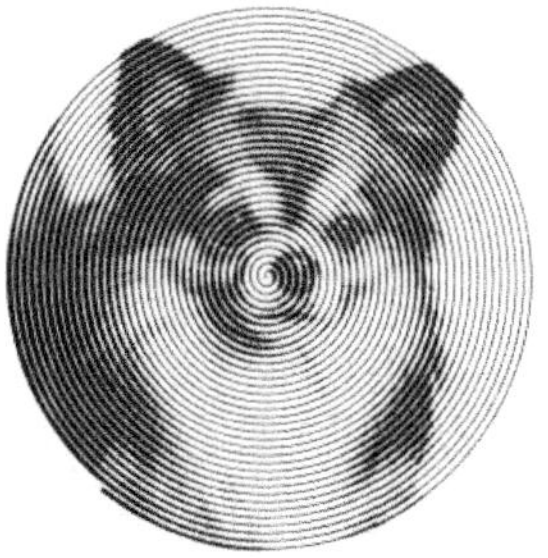

This page is intentionally left blank.

1

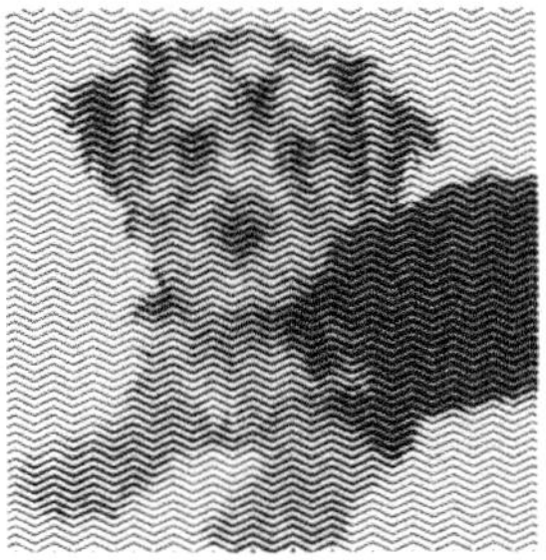

2

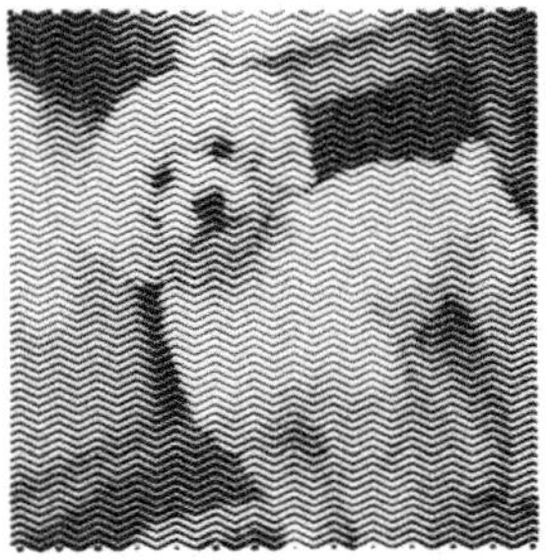

3

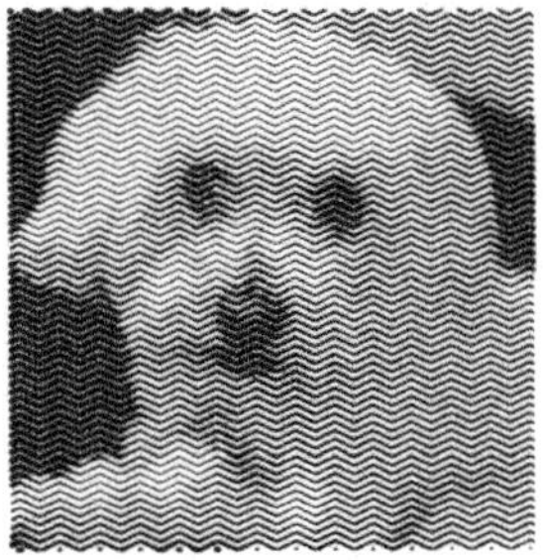

4

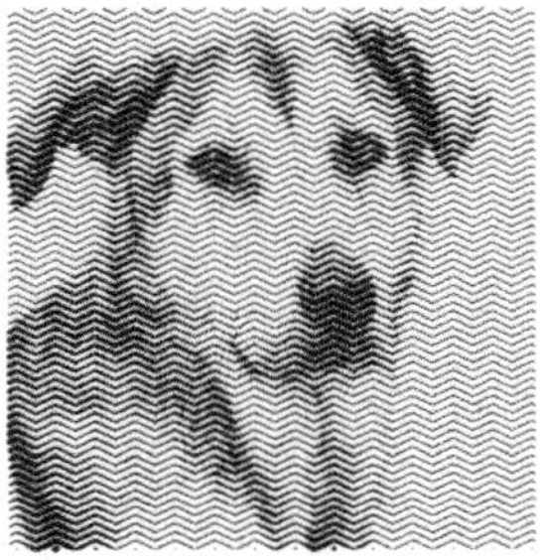

5

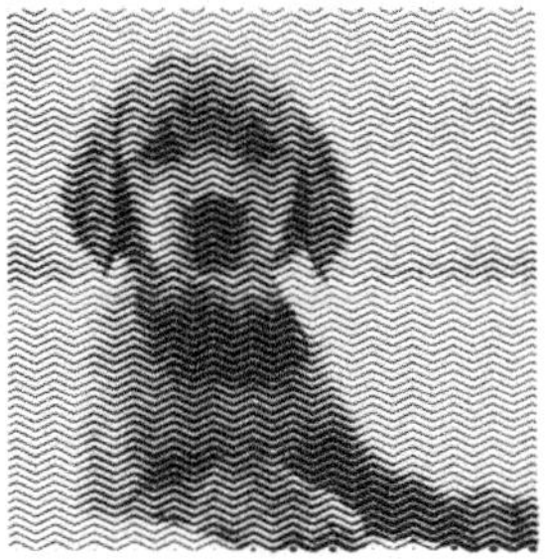

6

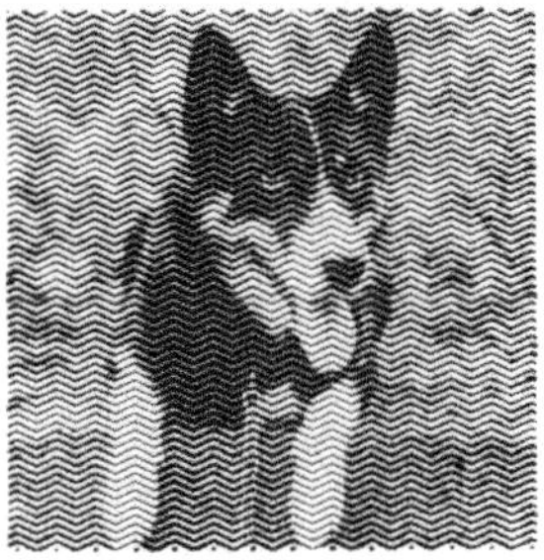

7

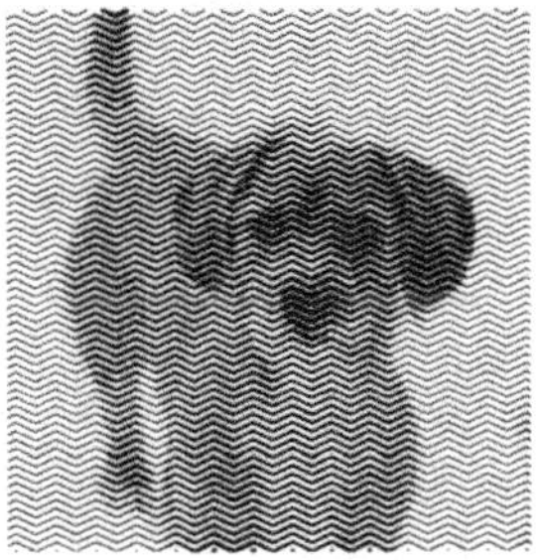

8

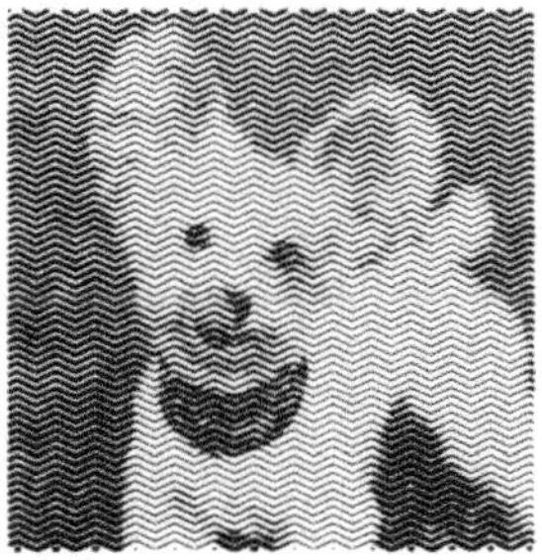

9

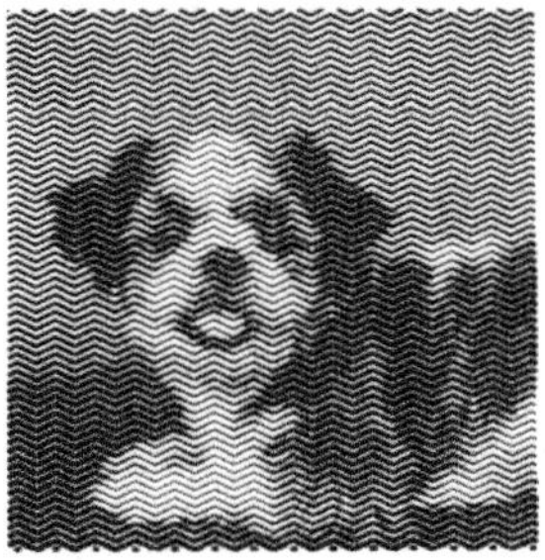

10

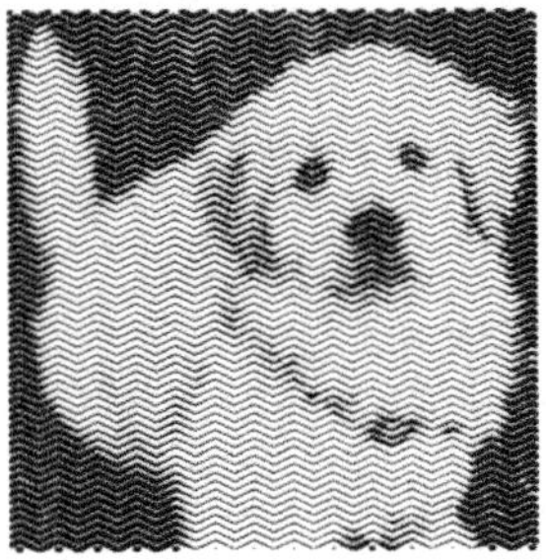

11

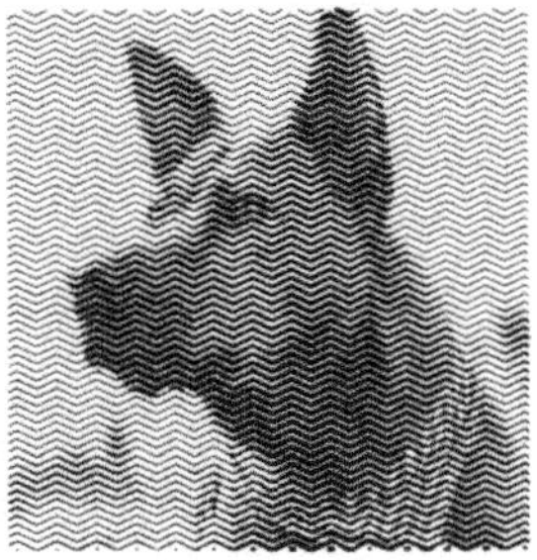

12

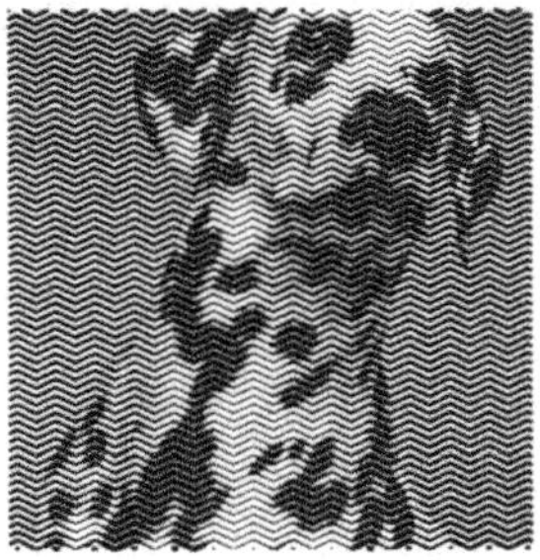

13

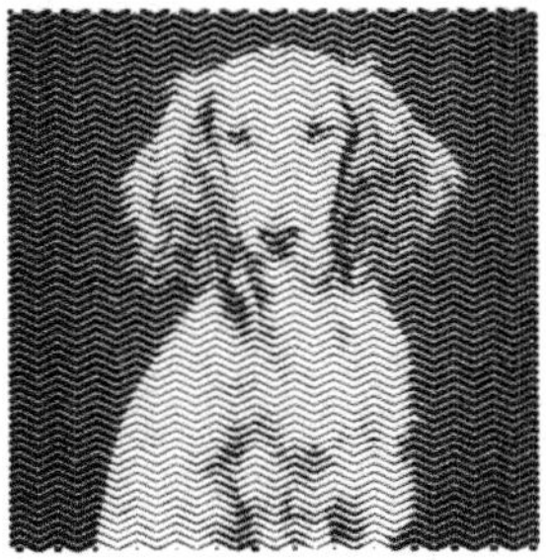

14

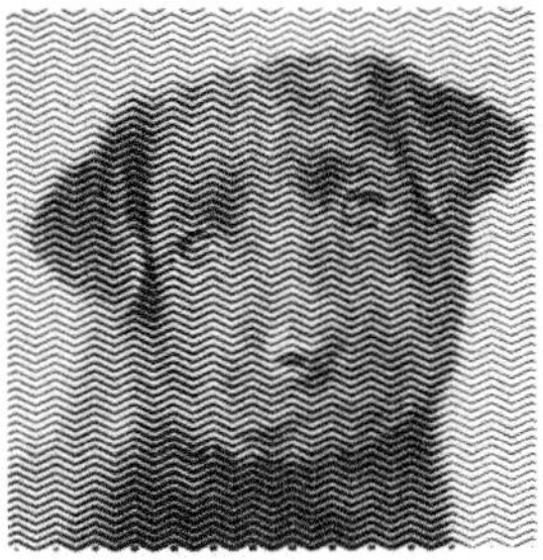

15

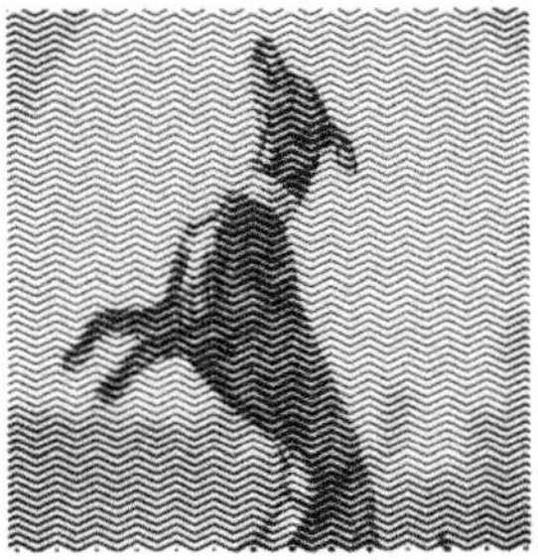

This page is intentionally left blank.

1

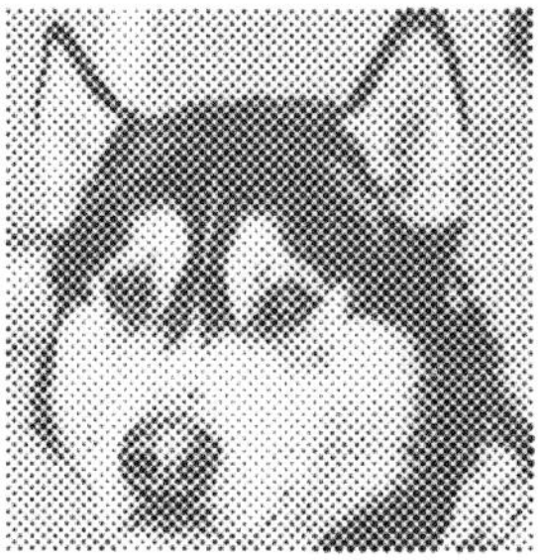

2

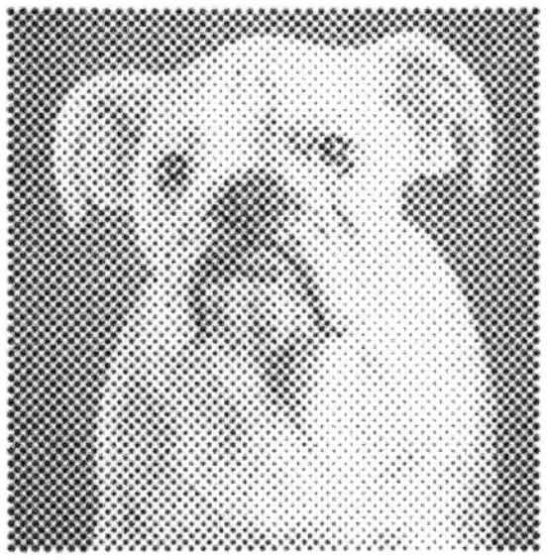

3

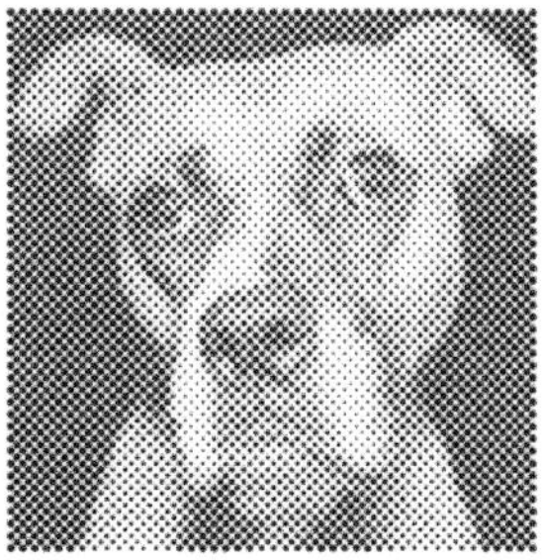

4

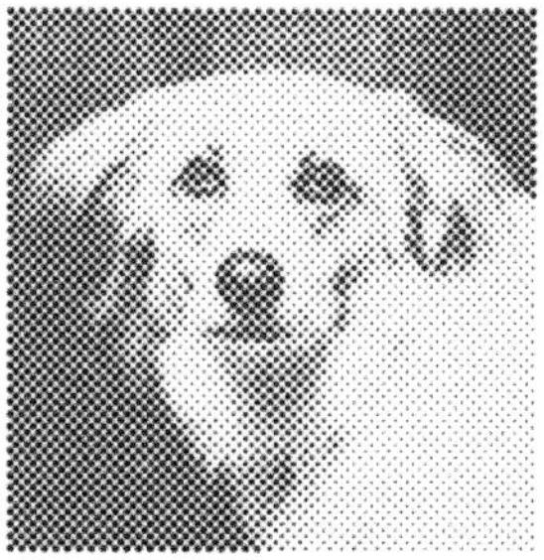

5

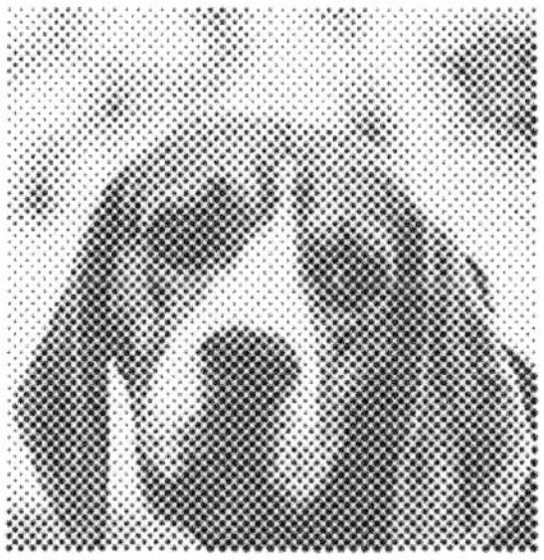

6

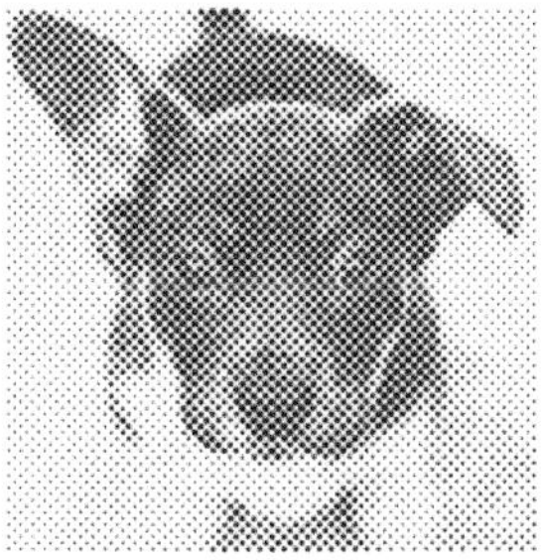

7

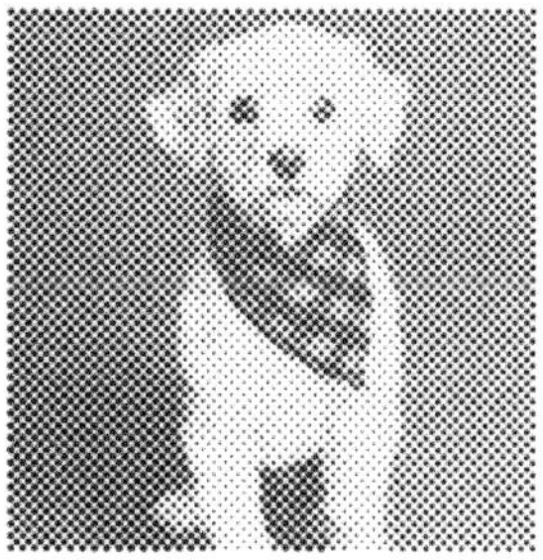

8

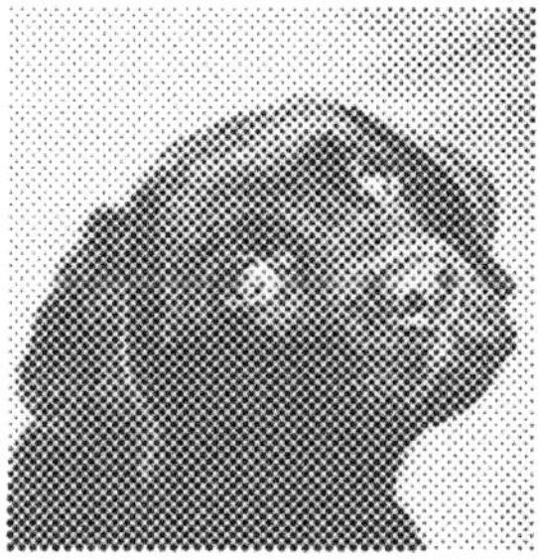

9

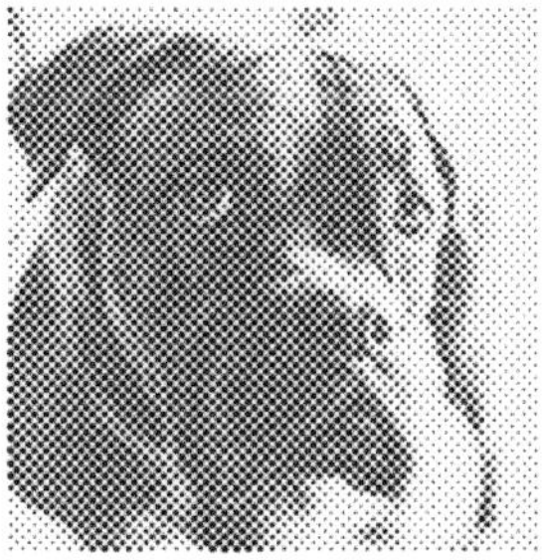

10

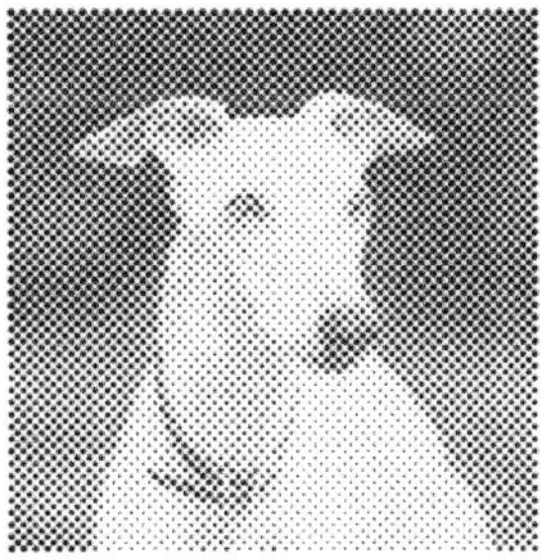

11

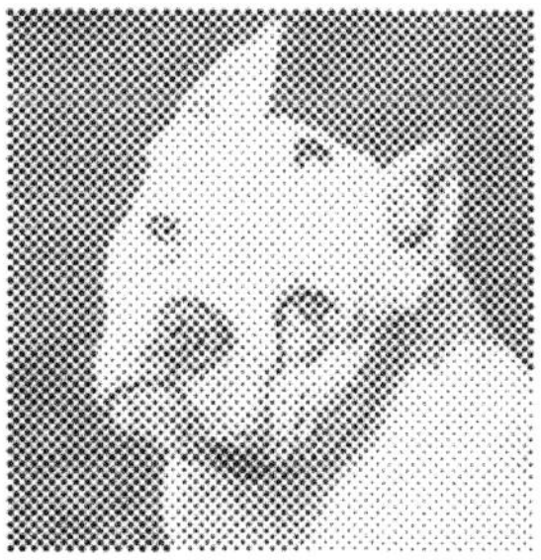

12

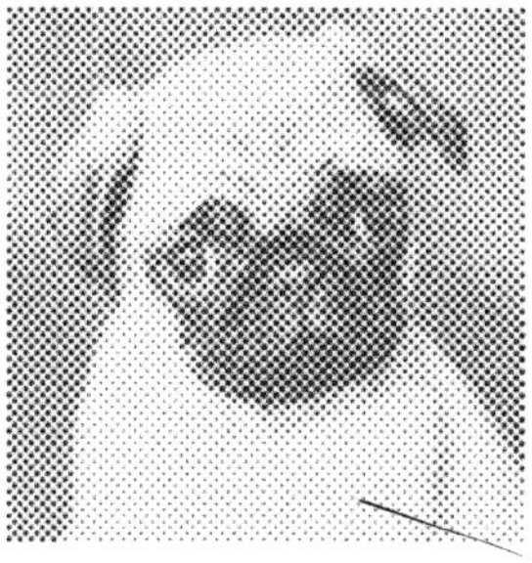

13

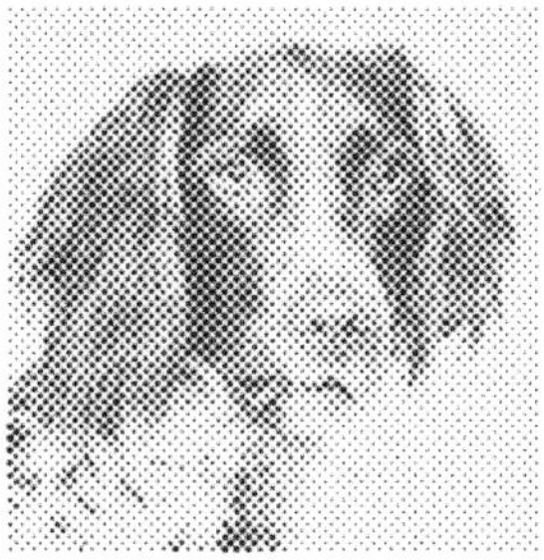

14

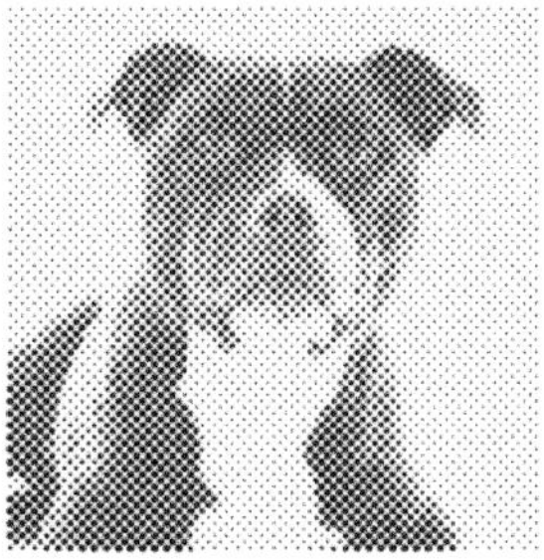

15

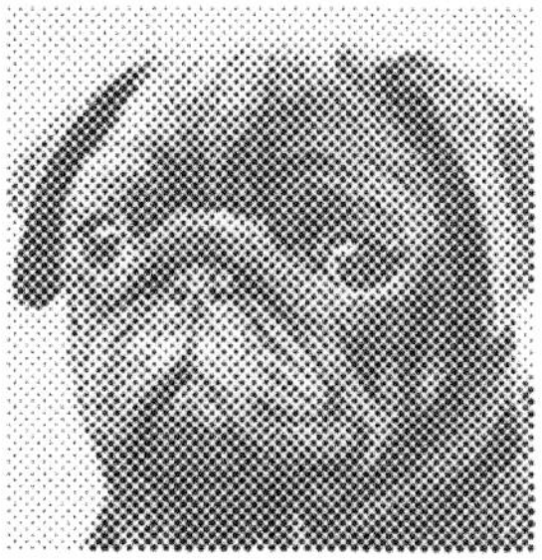

This page is intentionally left blank.

Buffer paper

Please cut and use between pages when you color with any ink that may cause bleeding.

This page is intentionally left blank.

Buffer paper

Please cut and use between pages when you color with any ink that may cause bleeding.

This page is intentionally left blank.

Printed in Great Britain
by Amazon